History in Living Memory

Home Life
Through the Years

How daily life
has changed in
living memory

Clare Lewis

raintree

a Capstone company — publishers for children

Raintree is an imprint of Capstone Global Library Limited, a company incorporated in England and Wales having its registered office at 7 Pilgrim Street, London, EC4V 6LB – Registered company number: 6695582

www.raintree.co.uk
myorders@raintree.co.uk

Edited by Clare Lewis and Holly Beaumont
Designed by Philippa Jenkins
Picture research by Tracy Cummins
Production by Victoria Fitzgerald
Originated by Capstone Global Library Ltd
Printed and bound in China by Leo Paper Group

ISBN 978 1 406 29014 1
18 17 16 15 14
10 9 8 7 6 5 4 3 2 1

British Library Cataloguing in Publication Data
A full catalogue record for this book is available from the British Library.

Acknowledgements
We would like to thank the following for permission to reproduce photographs: Alamy: © ClassicStock, 11, 13, 15; Capstone Press: Philippa Jenkins, 1 Top Left; Corbis: © Chuck Savage, 17; Corel: Arthur Beales, 4; Getty Images: f8 Imaging, 14, George Marks/Retrofile, 6, 7, 8; Glow Images: Superstock, 9; Shutterstock: Don Bendickson, 23 Bottom, Everett Collection, Cover Top, Flas100, Design Element, Hurst Photo, 22 Top Left, Lu Mikhaylova, 22 Bottom, merzzie, 20, Monkey Business Images, 21, Cover Bottom, olmarmar, 22 Top Right, Peter Gudella, 23 Top, SeDmi, 23 Middle, Studio DMM Photography, Designs & Art, Design Element; SuperStock: ClassicStock, 1 Bottom, Exactostock, 12, Superstock, 10; Thinkstock: Comstock, 16, Back Cover, 19, Fuse, 18; Wikimedia: Gizurr, 5.

Every effort has been made to contact copyright holders of material reproduced in this book. Any omissions will be rectified in subsequent printings if notice is given to the publisher.

All the internet addresses (URLs) given in this book were valid at the time of going to press. However, due to the dynamic nature of the internet, some addresses may have changed, or sites may have changed or ceased to exist since publication. While the author and publisher regret any inconvenience this may cause readers, no responsibility for any such changes can be accepted by either the author or the publisher.

Some words are shown in bold, **like this**. You can find them in the glossary on page 23.

Contents

What is history in living memory?

Some history happened a very long time ago. Nobody alive now lived through it.

Some history did not happen so long ago.
Our parents, grandparents and adult
friends can tell us how life used to be.
We call this history in living memory.

How has daily life changed in living memory?

When your grandparents were young, home life was quite different from now. For example, cleaning and cooking were hard work and took a long time.

Families had fun together, though, just like today. They listened to the radio and played board games.

How did people do housework in the 1950s?

In the 1950s, electricity in the home was quite new. Homes didn't have as many electric machines as they do today.

Most people didn't own a vacuum cleaner. People swept and mopped floors to keep them clean.

How did people shop in the 1960s?

People shopped for food more often in the 1960s than we do today. Shops were smaller and often nearer people's homes.

People walked to local shops to buy fresh food each day. Sometimes local shops would deliver food by bicycle.

How were people's homes heated in the past?

In the past, houses often had smaller rooms. These were heated with wood or **coal** fires.

In the 1960s, more people put **central heating** in their homes. This made houses warmer and more comfortable.

How did people prepare food in the 1970s?

In the 1970s, meals could take a long time to prepare. People did not buy as many **convenience foods** as they do now.

microwave oven

Microwave ovens began to be used in the 1970s. These helped people cook food more quickly.

How did shopping change in the 1980s?

In the 1980s, huge supermarkets were built. People drove to them to do their shopping.

Instead of shopping in a lot of different shops, people could now buy food, clothes and things for the home all in one place.

What were homes like in the 1990s?

People's homes had a lot of electrical gadgets by the 1990s. Dishwashers could do the washing-up after meals. Washing machines could wash clothes.

More people started to have computers at home. They used them for work and for fun.

What is your home life like today?

Some things are very different from when your grandparents were young. For example, you probably have many more electric machines in your kitchen.

Some things are not so different.
People still like to spend time cooking.
Families still have fun playing games
together at home.

Picture quiz

Which of these were used to clean things in the home in the 1950s?

broom

mop

vacuum cleaner

Do we still use them today?

22

Picture glossary

central heating
system for heating houses where hot water is sent through pipes to radiators in each room

coal
hard black rock that is dug out of the ground. It burns well.

convenience foods
food that is already prepared and ready to cook or eat

Find out more

Books

Houses and Homes (Ways into History),
  Sally Hewitt (Franklin Watts, 2012)
Washing and Cleaning (Comparing Past and Present),
  Rebecca Rissman (Raintree, 2014)

Website
**www.bbc.co.uk/schoolradio/subjects/history/
britainsince1930s**
Listen to audio clips and take a look at transport and
technology since the 1930s.

Index